A Frying Pan is Not a Gift

A Frying Pan is Not a Gift

Helpful Hints for Staying Married and Raising a ~~Somewhat~~ Happy Family For At Least 32 Years

Bob Borneman

Copyright © 2011 Bob Borneman

All rights reserved. No part of this book may be used or reproduced by any means, graphic, electronic, or mechanical, including photocopying, recording, taping or by any information storage retrieval system without the written permission of the publisher except in the case of brief quotations embodied in critical articles and reviews.

WestBow Press books may be ordered through booksellers or by contacting:

WestBow Press
A Division of Thomas Nelson
1663 Liberty Drive
Bloomington, IN 47403
www.westbowpress.com
1-(866) 928-1240

Because of the dynamic nature of the Internet, any web addresses or links contained in this book may have changed since publication and may no longer be valid. The views expressed in this work are solely those of the author and do not necessarily reflect the views of the publisher, and the publisher hereby disclaims any responsibility for them.

Any people depicted in stock imagery provided by Thinkstock are models, and such images are being used for illustrative purposes only.

Certain stock imagery © Thinkstock.

ISBN: 978-1-4497-3230-1 (sc)
ISBN: 978-1-4497-3231-8 (e)

Library of Congress Control Number: 2011961171

Printed in the United States of America

WestBow Press rev. date: 11/23/2011

To my sons, Adam, Will and Walker, in the hope that they will keep the wife they started with by not causing her to run away.

And to Koelling, my daughter, in the hope she will find a man that will love her as much as I do.

But most of all, to my wife Mary Dell, without whose love, friendship, humor and constant feedback, this work could not have happened, literally.

Table of Contents

Preface xi

Forward xiii

Living With Your Wife 1
    The Other 5 Commandments 1
    Quiet Fighting 2
    Blissitudology 2
    Home Cookin' 2
    R-E-S-P-E-C-T 2
    Go Team! 3
    Listen Up! 3
    Nap Time 3
    Nesting 4
    Homework 4
    Dating 4
    The Big Night Out 5
    The Getaway 5
    Present Situation 6
    Getting Carded 6
    Flowers 6
    Recreational Shopping 6
    The Perfect Gift 7
    Beauty Queen 9
    BFsF 10

And Then There Were Kids 11
    Kid Sit 11
    Day Care 12
    Vacation Time 12
    Sons 13
    Daughters 14
    Cain't Get No Respect 15
    Not So Heavy Hitter 15
    Their "Friends" 16
    This Too Shall Pass 17
    Parenting the Hard Way 18
    Hard to Like 18
    You are a Kid in Your Family Too 19
    Silent Sunday 19
    Driver's Ed 21
    Sports Phenom 22
    Leader of the Pack 23

Money, or the Lack Thereof 25
    It Builds Character 25
    Who's In Charge? 25
    The High Cost of Affection 25
    House of Cards 26
    Credit Rating 26
    Insurance 27
    Home Buying 28
    Save A Little 28
    Maintenance Man 29
    Don't Rent 29
    Tithing, Or Some Semblance Thereof 30

You Da' Man	31
You Time	31
Sneak Attack	32
Walk the Talk	32
Church is Good	33
Framily	34
In Conclusion	35
Glossary	37
About The Author	39

Preface

There is a big difference between wisdom and knowledge. Knowledge is what you get from reading books, going to school (if you stay awake) and touching the stove to see if it is hot, even though it is glowing red. Wisdom is correctly answering the question from your wife "Honey, do these jeans make my butt look big?" If you have not yet attained wisdom, the answer to this question is **not** "No honey, it ain't the jeans; it's that bag of Oreos you ate last night."

Since the average marriage only lasts 8 years, I feel blessed to still be married to the same person for 32 years (and counting). Both my parents and my wife's parents never divorced. I do recall my father in-law stating on the occasion of his 50th wedding anniversary, "I have never considered divorce; murder possibly, but never divorce." Humor runs deep and wide throughout our family.

I am writing this book to my children, especially the boys so they will not make some of the same mistakes I made when trying to learn how to be married. This little book is my feeble attempt to impart some of the wisdom I have gained in 32 years of marriage to a wonderful wife, soul mate, friend, lover, mother of my children, and center of my universe, in the hope that all of my boys will keep the wife they started with and will raise a family they can be proud of.

Forward

"A Frying Pan Is Not a Gift" is an enigma! Bob, the author, is a Forestry Major with a Masters in Decision Science, neither of which has anything to do with writing a book. I, on the other hand, have a Journalism Degree. I have writing coursing through my veins. I honed this gift in college with pen and paper, writing until my fingers bled, preparing myself to write for my supper. There were no computers. I cut and pasted the old fashioned way, with scissors and Elmer's glue. I've even suffered "writer's block" while paying bills. I've written nothing but checks, notes to teachers and a poem to the tune of "There Is Nothing Like A Dame" for my mother's 80th birthday.

After reading "A Frying Pan Is Not A Gift" it is apparent to me that while I was otherwise occupied being married and pregnant, raising a family, being pregnant, bagging groceries at night, being pregnant, working retail at night, substitute teaching, chasing after my elusive sanity, and being pregnant again, Bob was surreptitiously taking notes for his book. Now, after almost 33 years of marital blissitudology (it's in the book), he wants to share what he has learned at my expense and under my tutelage. I feel like a science fair project. I'm quite pleased with the way our experiment turned out but I'm stunned to discover how much there was to be taught, how long it took him to become proficient in some areas and just how little men really know before they mumble "I do". We should probably consider changing that to "I do…. But how?"

I do really love this book. I want to integrate into marriage vows, "with this book I thee wed". There are that many good hard learned lessons that would benefit any marriage. Bob's advice is supported by 32 years of "research and development" in a mostly blissful marriage. Over the past 7 years when family and friends have had a chance to read the original version of this book their response is always, "you should publish this". So he did, and as you read "A Frying Pan Is Not A Gift", you will see where our own bumps in the road have come from over the years, why he is a great dad, and why I felt incredibly blessed when he said "I do" to me, and loved me enough to figure out the "how". Enjoy!

Mary Dell Borneman

Living With Your Wife

The Other 5 Commandments

I. You must love your wife with all of your heart, more than yourself, and even your mother.

II. Humor is important in a marriage. If you can make your wife laugh, it will endear you to her. All people naturally want to be around someone who makes them laugh.

III. Marriages seem to work best when both spouses give to the other more than they receive.

IV. Never tell your wife you are disappointed in her. It is worse than saying you hate her.

V. Never introduce your spouse as, "This is my first wife…"

Quiet Fighting

If you have noticed that your wife has not talked to you in several hours and seems to be ignoring you, this is usually an indication that you are having a fight. It is your job to figure out what you did and then apologize for it as sincerely as you can. If you can't figure out what you did, at least apologize for making her upset with you. If you are not the one at fault, apologize anyway—she is not going to, and one of you has to.

Blissitudology

You have heard it said, "If Momma ain't happy, ain't nobody happy." I tell you that this especially applies to wives. There will be no peace until you figure out what happened and do all in your power to rectify it. This is called Blissitudology, which is the study of domestic bliss-making. It could possibly be something that did *not* happen that caused the unhappiness. If so, make it happen.

Home Cookin'

Never compare your wife's cooking to your mother's cooking. Your wife's cooking is always excellent. If you think otherwise, don't say anything unless you want her to stop cooking altogether, because that is what is going to happen if you say anything negative. Freezer food can get old fairly quickly, and eating out is expensive.

R-E-S-P-E-C-T

Respect your wife. Respect comes in many forms—here are a few:

- Your wife is not your mother. Clean up after yourself.
- Put your dirty laundry in the hamper; don't leave it on the floor.

- Wash any dishes you use, and if there are other dishes in the sink, wash them too.
- It is as much your job to do the dishes as it is your wife's.
- Ask her opinion.
- Involve her in your life.

Go Team!

Having a wife and family requires teamwork. Sometimes there will be two teams—on one team is you and your wife; on the other is your kids. As teammates, you and your wife need to help each other out and be on the same page regarding things like punishment of the kids, rules for the kids, and faith for the family. If you are not on the same page, the other team being clever, will notice and use it against you. You also need to help each other out as teammates around the house. One teammate will be really good at fixing things; the other will be good at making things look better. Some things either teammate can do well, so if it needs doing, take the initiative and do it without being asked. These are things like dishes, yard work, cleaning up, and laundry.

Listen Up!

Everything your wife says is important—sometimes just not at that particular moment. Sometimes it's hard to follow, however. My wife has this habit of branching when telling her stories. It's kind of like listening to a story with an unlimited number of subplots. Nonetheless, when your wife is speaking to you, look her in the eyes, and really listen to what she is saying.

Nap Time

Never fall asleep while your wife is talking to you. I actually did this *once*. She was more upset than I thought necessary. Looking back, however, it was probably one of the most insulting things I have ever done to her. It's like saying, "What you have to say is so unimportant, I think I will just take a nap while you tell me."

Nesting

Your wife has a need to make a nice home for her family, which usually includes you. Let her do it. It will cost a lot of money. You will buy things that have no functional value but are either sweet or cute. She may ask your opinion—say whatever you want, but she is going to buy it anyway. In the end, you will have a home that you will be proud to show your visitors.

Homework

The Ten Commandments include keeping the Sabbath holy. The same commandment also says that you will work six days, not just five. That sixth day should be spent working around the house. A very genuine way to show your wife how much you love her is to help her care for your home. It is wise not to spend that sixthday with the guys playing golf or softball, especially if there are kids at home. Your wife will pretend not to care, but deep down, she really resents it.

Dating

Date your wife. This will be easy in the early years before kids come along. It is much more important after the kids come along. If your wife is keeping the kids at home all day every day, she really needs adult interaction, and this can include you. It can be simple—even just a pizza or an egg roll.

The Big Night Out

Your wife loves to dress up and go to fancy places to eat and act sophisticated. You may think she doesn't care, and she may even say so. At least once a year, take her somewhere very nice and preferably expensive. If you are adventurous, throw in some dancing. Your wife will be even more flattered if she knows you really hate doing this kind of stuff under normal circumstances. On the date, be extremely courteous, and use your best manners.

The Getaway

Take your wife away for the weekend at least once a year—twice is better—without the kids. We try to do this around our anniversary. We were cruel to our parents and got married on December 15. We like to go to the north Georgia mountains for our anniversary. Often when we get to our destination, we are practically the only ones there. A couple of times it has snowed, and once it snowed so much we had to stay an extra day—dang it! A getaway is a wonderful time, and it will rekindle your relationship.

Present Situation

If your wife ever tells you, "Let's not get anything for each other for Christmas this year," don't believe it for a second. She is going to get you something. You better have something to give her as well. The trick is figuring out how much to spend. She will feel bad if she gets you something small and you get something big, and vice versa. My best advice is to get two gifts and let her give hers first. You can always return one of the gifts.

Getting Carded

Give your wife a card, at the very least, for every occasion that requires one: birthday, Mother's Day, Valentine's Day, your anniversary, and Christmas. Take some time to choose a card that has some significance for you and your wife. Don't get a generic card, because she will know you did not put any effort into it and that you forgot until the last minute. Flowers are a nice touch as well.

Flowers

Give your wife flowers occasionally for absolutely no reason. Do not expect anything in return from this gesture.

Recreational Shopping

Occasionally your wife may ask you to go shopping with her. It is a great way to spend time with your wife. Hopefully you will be talking to each other by the time you get home. What your wife wants to do is what I call "recreational shopping." Recreational shopping involves browsing through stores with no particular items in mind to purchase. I find it is best to think of recreational shopping as a date with your wife. With that frame of mind, you really can have a good time. You can buy some coffee and meander through a variety of shops and hopefully walk out with all the money you went in with.

If your wife is from the South, you may also discover she has a lot of new friends after a day of shopping. One such trip occurred when we were browsing through a gift shop in Rome, Georgia. Before we left the shop we knew where the shop owner's family was from, who her kids were, where they lived, and where they are now. Likewise the shop owner now knows all of our kids, where they live and where we live. All this at a cost of only $44.39! I think they pinky-pledged to stay in touch.

Without the date frame of mind, you are likely to exhibit some behaviors that will annoy your wife and bring an end to what could have been a good day. Some of the behaviors to avoid are:

- Standing by the door looking at your watch
- Leaning on the register waiting for her to check out
- Sitting in the car while she is in the shop
- Acting like you would rather be somewhere else.

Your role as a participant in the recreational shopping date is to have fun, be engaging and provide funding if necessary. The date can also double as a gift-giving opportunity.

The Perfect Gift

The trick to successful gift-giving to your wife is to find something that has some sentimental value between you and her. I am still working on it—this is what I have figured out so far.

It is very difficult to buy clothes for your wife and I would highly recommend avoiding it, unless of course you feel you are stylish enough to handle it. Here are some other things you should NEVER buy for your wife:

- Exercise equipment
- A frying pan
- Lawn equipment (gardening equipment is OK, if she likes gardening)
- Any kind of "How To" book
- Scrapbook making supplies
- Household appliances (such as a vacuum cleaner or toaster oven)
- Tools
- Pets

Some things your wife will likely enjoy getting from you include:

- Jewelry
- Antiques
- Jewelry
- Pearls
- Jewelry
- A Framed picture of your family
- A Watch or bracelet
- Electronic gadgetry—if it's fun, like an iPod or iPad, but not a calculator

Beauty Queen

Tell your wife how beautiful she is. The more you tell her she is beautiful, the more beautiful she will become. You have to be sincere however. Telling her she's beautiful when she has just come in from gardening or after running 5 miles does not work. The best time is when she is dressed for work or church. You should never use the word cute as that description is reserved for children and puppies.

BFsF

If you are very lucky your wife will have a few best girlfriends she can talk to. There are many girl things that your wife will not want to discuss with you. Make sure you allow your wife to spend time with these friends by taking care of the kids or whatever is needed to free up some of her time. In the end you will benefit from this.

And Then There Were Kids

Kid Sit

Never refer to watching after your own children as babysitting. This is an easy trap to fall into. I should know since I have made this mistake far too many times. For some reason my wife is convinced that watching your own kids is different than babysitting someone else's kids. My opinion is that everyone's kids do the same things and you have to yell the same threats to all of them. I think the only difference between babysitting your own kids and babysitting someone else's kids is that changing someone else's kid's dirty diaper is a lot grosser than changing your own kid's dirty diaper. My wife's opinion is that what you are doing with your own kids is known as parenting.

Day Care

We have been very blessed to be able to have my wife at home raising our kids while they were young. As they have grown older and we have only one high school kid left, she has returned to work (at his school). Keeping kids at home is a lot harder than going to an office and going to work. Try it for a few days if you doubt it. Kids have a lot of energy and they like to expend it. Kids can also tell when their parents are getting tired, and that's when they really pour it on. If you are like me, you will be dying to go back to work and deal with the grownup kids there.

Vacation Time

Take the whole family on a vacation at least once a year. You will have to work hard to find cheap places to go, but the memories that come from these trips are priceless. Camping can be a good way to go here. We have been going on vacations with the whole family since we have had kids. We continue the tradition now, even though three of the four of them no longer live with us (they are grown, and *no* we did not sell them or put them up for adoption). It's really a lot of fun to spend time with your grown up kids. Guess what, sometimes they offer to pay for dinner or drinks!

Sons

If you have a son, make sure he grows up knowing he is a boy. Play rough with him. Play sports with him. Play outdoors with him. Just play with him. Make sure he knows he can come to you with his problems.

Bob Borneman

Daughters

If you have a daughter, make sure she knows she is a girl. Your wife will have to help you with this. Play with her, play house, have tea parties, play with her stuffed animals, play softball, be part of her world. Love your daughter by protecting her, listening to her, and hugging her. Make sure she knows she can come to you with her problems.

Cain't Get No Respect

It is important for your kids to respect you, so don't do anything that would cause this to not happen. The surest way to lose respect from your kids is to engage in any of the following: infidelity, drunkenness, lying (even a little), cheating (even a little), laziness or anything that would embarrass them if their friends find out about it.

Not So Heavy Hitter

Never, ever hit your kids. I know old school child punishment was useful for some parents, but for me it was difficult. It seemed to work well years ago in High School if I remember correctly. Our assistant principal had a paddle with holes in it. He said the holes made it more aerodynamic so he could get more velocity on his forehand stroke. Of course I just heard about it, I never got paddled.

There is a difference between spanking and hitting. Spanking is done as a form of punishment or to immediately stop a behavior your child is exhibiting. Hitting is done out of anger, and usually results in remorse. I hit one of my sons *once*. I remember seeing the outline of my five-fingered hand on his bare rear end. He was a little guy at the time. I got sick to my stomach. When they get to be teenagers, you cannot hit them hard enough to make a difference anyway and sometimes they hit back. What I do find effective is yelling at them as loud as you can to the point that they think you have gone crazy. Fear is a more useful tool for me.

Their "Friends"

Your kids will have friends, and there's very little you can do to stop it. These friends will take your place at some point as the most important people in their lives. That point seems to be around middle school. Not being the center of their universe will break your heart but it is unavoidable. My wife and I liked most of our kids' friends. There were a couple of them that were downright scary. I imagine that some of them are either in jail or well on their way. One of the scariest was a guy we called "Death Metal Dan", who ended up being a Marine and is now a policeman and a super nice respectable guy. Most of the rest of them were harmless. They would just swoop in like locusts and clean out our refrigerator for us. One of them came over for a visit one afternoon and outstayed his welcome. I was a little perturbed when I was off to work, my wife was getting kids off to school and the "friend" was in his underwear in our living room playing PlayStation games. I had to have my son ask him to leave after 5 days.

A Frying Pan is Not a Gift

There is a fine line between wanting to provide a safe, fun and loving environment for your kids' friends, and enabling them to escape from problems at their homes.

Take heart in the fact that as your kids get close to adulthood, they become your friends again. They also begin to understand how right you were about pretty much everything.

This Too Shall Pass

Your kids will disappoint you at times. You will think you did such a great job raising such a mature and sophisticated kid, and then they will do something incredibly stupid, possibly expensive and likely destructive. In our family, these incidents often involved cars, those friends I mentioned before and Acute Severe Obnoxious Behavior (A-SOB). One particular time the police were involved. When I got the call from the police to go to the scene of the incident, I was incredibly angry. When I got there, I saw my car resting against a brick mailbox.

The passenger window was shattered. The trunk lid was open and there was a case of toilet paper in it. I started screaming as loud as possible to all involved, and actually scared the policeman who got in his patrol car and said it looked like I had it under control.

Remember, it is nothing you didn't do as a kid, and you also lived through it. It is a part of growing up.

Parenting the Hard Way

You need to let your kids make mistakes. You will know the consequences of what they are doing are going to be painful to them. They however are not going to listen to you because they know better and their friends are all doing it. As long as the consequences are not life-threatening, involve jail time or permanently harm other people, let them make the mistake. Later you can take pleasure in the "I told you so" that you are entitled to give them.

Hard to Like

Sometimes it is really hard to like your kids, even though you really love them. During the high school years your kids may say some heartbreaking things to you. Things like "I hate living here" and "Why are you always nagging me?" and "I hate coming home." This is the sign that your child is making the transition from your home to moving out into the world. You should try to avoid the temptation of helping them move out by putting all of their things in a suitcase out at the end of the driveway for them to find when they come home from school. Though this act may make you feel good in the short run, it could do long term damage to your relationship with your child.

We do the same rebellious things to God as His children. I think when your children act this way, it is God's way of reminding us how patient He is with us.

You are a Kid in Your Family Too

Like it or not your parents and your in-laws are also part of your family. It is sometimes difficult to find time for your parents in your life. You will finally realize why God had to make one of the Ten Commandments to honor your father and your mother— it does not come easily. Making time for your parents becomes very difficult when kids come along and the holiday season approaches. You will find yourself driving to both parents' houses and eating multiple large meals a day. Know that your parents appreciate this, they went through it too, and they are not going to cut you any slack.

Silent Sunday

Sunday has always been a special day at our house. It was the one day we *tried* to relax. Sometimes our kids had a Sunday agenda that would be different than ours. When my older sons were in high school,

they started a band… in our basement.

It is an unwritten rule in the rock and roll world that the house where band practice happens is the house where the drummer lives. This was our house. We had a drummer and a guitarist in the band. It probably would have been tolerable if it had been normal rock and roll music, but our boys were (and still are) heavy metal enthusiasts.

A typical Sunday would include getting all the kids ready for church, going to church, going out for lunch afterwards and then changing our clothes to sit down and relax or take a nap. Then later in the afternoon

we would be serenaded by the band playing Metallica songs and homemade death metal songs. If you have never heard homemade death metal, imagine yourself standing about 5 feet from a railroad track. There are two freight trains coming down the track at 60 miles per hour, one from each direction. They collide right in front of where you are standing. The sound that you would hear would be similar to what was coming out of our basement on a Sunday afternoon.

It is important to support your kids in their endeavors. We always wanted to provide our kids opportunities to explore whatever interested them. However, there are times when you have to draw the line, so we invoked the "Silent Sunday" rule. Silent Sunday was our attempt to make at least one day of the week a time for rest and relaxation. No band practice on Sunday when there are six other days of the week for practice. Silent Sunday encompasses more than just the band. The other Silent Sunday rules include no lawn mowing, weed eating, or other motorized noise around the house. Silent Sunday lives on in our house today; everyone knows that noisy activities must be done on Saturday. Silent Sunday rocks!

Driver's Ed

One of the scariest propositions facing any parent is teaching your children to operate two tons of steel traveling at 70 miles per hour while they are strapped inside it. Driving a car is further complicated by fun distractions like radios, iPods, cell phones and friends. It's never too early to start the driver's education process; I generally started around age 3, driving in the neighborhood. When they have reached the age where they can get a learner's permit, the serious training begins. All of my children drove a minimum of 1,000 miles with me in the car before they could take the test to get a real driver's license. Since it will take you about 25 hours of driving to go 1,000 miles, it is also a great way to spend time with your teenager. You may even discover that you actually like some of the music your child listens to.

Bob Borneman

Sports Phenom

My kid is awesome at sports. Why can't everyone see that? Why won't they let him play so they can see how awesome he is? I think I will get him some lessons; it's a great deal for only $75 for a half hour. Better yet, I will coach my own team so I can make sure my kid plays all the time. Then, we will join a travel team for 7 year olds so people in other places can see how awesome he is. After that, the high school coaches will all beg him to transfer to their school district so he can play on their team. Of course, he will be able to go to college for free, which will make the 12 years and $25,000 investment worth it.

If you have said or thought anything like this, like I have, it's time to wake up and smell the cleats. Speaking from the experience of having my kids play sports for the past 21 years (and counting), your child could possibly be a phenomenon in your own mind only. It's a natural thing to think your kid is better than the others (especially if they are). Other parents are thinking the same thing about their kid as well.

Your kid may actually be good when young, but as they grow up, they will change physically and their abilities will change with them. Sometimes they get much better and sometimes they peak when young. I have seen kids who couldn't run or catch, who now play baseball in college. I have seen home run kings at age 12, who did not make their high school team. Sometimes they get hurt and can no longer play. In high school they may have a boyfriend or girlfriend and lose interest in sports. For one of our sons it was a high school coach who was so miserable some kids left for another high school, and others, like ours, just decided not to play anymore. Another one of our sons is headed off to play baseball in college.

The best thing you can do for your athletic prodigy is to make sure they are having fun. Be supportive, but not oppressive. You want them to have fun so they will continue playing. You want them to continue playing, because it makes them tired and occupies their spare time which in turn keeps them out of trouble. An additional benefit is that their teammates are probably going to be their best friends, and generally they are really good kids.

Leader of the Pack

It is important to your wife that you appear to be head of the household. She may think she is, but when the tough decisions come, you will need to be where the buck stops. It is a huge responsibility, but that is why you are the man of the family and why God designed it that way. You will likely find that when the going gets tough, your wife does not want to take responsibility for the big decisions, and she should not have too, unless you are a sniveling wimp. When you do make that big decision, and if things go badly, take responsibility for it. Conversely, if things go well, you get the credit. Be humble, however.

Kids do not get to make decisions. Mom and Dad get to make their decisions for them. They will not like it sometimes, and they will ask

"Why can't I stay out until 4:00 am?" You don't have to provide a long explanation as an answer to this question, you can simply say, "It's not a good idea, and you are not doing it." They need to learn to trust that you have their best interest at heart. Of course it's always great when one of the other kids who did stay out until 4:00 am gets into some trouble and has to deal with it.

Money, or the Lack Thereof

It Builds Character

There will be no extra money for many years when you are first married. Think of this as a character building experience. Having no money is very stressful. Do not fall into the temptation of blaming your spouse for financial problems. There is almost always something you can do without to save some money. Later in life when you start to have a few dollars, you will appreciate more the things you have, and will take better care of them.

Who's In Charge?

You may consider letting your wife handle the finances in your home. There is an upside and a downside to this. The upside is that she is likely the one who will be doing all the shopping, so it makes sense for her to know how much money there is and where it is located. The downside is that you may not know how much money there is or where it is located. If you go this route, I recommend having at least some of your money deducted from your paycheck and put into an account that you can easily access. You are going to need this money for gifts for your wife.

The High Cost of Affection

Kids are expensive. The only cheap part of having kids is the actual conception. Immediately after that the bills start rolling in. They cost more as the years go by, and generally the increase in expense rises faster than your paycheck. Hopefully they will eventually get off your payroll. This should normally occur at college graduation or marriage, whichever comes first. We have been very fortunate so far. Of our four kids, three are independent, and the last one leaves for college next year. I am hoping to start seriously saving for retirement before I actually get to retirement.

House of Cards

Avoid credit cards if possible. If you must have one, make sure to pay off the entire balance when the bill comes in. The cards are designed to never be paid off if you only pay the minimum balance. The credit card is not free money; it is an expensive loan from a bank. I think I am still paying for my honeymoon.

There are different kinds of credit cards. Some credit cards will offer loyalty points that you can save up and use to buy merchandise, or even get a check back at the end of the year. These types of cards generally have higher interest rates. Other cards have no loyalty points, but usually have slightly lower interest rates. If you are able to pay off the entire balance every month, a loyalty type card is better. If you are going to have to make payments and keep a balance, the lower interest rate card is better.

Credit Rating

You will more than likely have to borrow money for the major purchases of life like houses and cars. I was so impressed by my grandfather who never had a loan, even to buy his first house. He was the first generation American of an Italian immigrant family. As such, money was hard to come by and loans to Italian farmers were virtually non-existent. He saved his money and did a lot of the work himself.

Since you will need to borrow money, it is very important that you have a good credit rating. Every person who has borrowed money has a credit rating that is calculated by a couple of companies who provide credit rating services to banks and car dealers. You want to have a good credit rating so you can get the best annual percentage rate when you borrow money. The higher the percentage rate, the more your monthly payments will be. Your credit rating is affected by how much you borrow and how you pay it back.

Things that negatively affect your credit rating:
- Borrowing too much money
- Not making payments when they are due
- Keeping the balances on your credit cards close to the limit
- Going over the credit limit

Things that positively affect your credit rating:
- Having one or two credit cards only
- Keeping the balance you owe relatively low compared to the limit
- Making the monthly payment before the due date
- Not going over the credit limit
- Paying off the entire balance every month

Insurance

You do not need life insurance if your wife is working and you do not have children. When you become the primary breadwinner of the family, you should have life insurance to make sure your family can survive without you. Term life is the cheapest. You need approximately ten times your annual salary in coverage. You can reduce the amount of insurance when your kids become of legal age. If you feel like you want to buy a whole life type of policy, get one with vanishing premiums so it will pay itself off and maintain the coverage.

Home Buying

Owning a home is better than renting a home. The interest portion of your house payment is tax deductible. This tax savings will usually make your net house payment cheaper than renting. Avoid adjustable rate mortgages when buying a house. They will lure you into buying more house than you can actually afford. Your house payment should be no more than one third of your gross monthly income to live comfortably.

Save A Little

Try to start a savings account while you are young. Have the money deducted from your paycheck and put directly into your savings account before you can get to it. If you do this, you will not miss it. You may decide to start saving for your children's' college education by starting a 529 plan for them. The 529 plan is a good way to have money automatically deducted from your account, and saved in an investment account. You are not allowed to use the money until you are making payments for college education. There are tax advantages to the 529 plan account as well.

If your employer offers a 401K plan retirement account, you should take advantage of it. It is a great way to save automatically and earn interest. Many employers also contribute to your account as well. If you leave the employer where you had a 401K, open an IRA (individual retirement account) and do a tax free rollover of your 401K into the IRA. The IRA is not associated with an employer, like the 401K is, so you it will stay with you when you change jobs.

Maintenance Man

If you learn to do your own home and car repairs you will save many thousands of dollars over the years. My working theory is that if the guy down at the garage can figure out how to fix cars, I should be able to figure it out as well. Buy yourself one of those automobile repair books down at the auto parts store. Become good buddies with your auto parts guy and he can help you by answering questions and making suggestions. If you really get into trouble, you can always have the thing towed to the mechanic, and they can fix it up for you. At least you tried.

Don't Rent

Owning is always better than renting, whether it is a car or a house. Rent payments never end. With ownership, there is a point that you will actually own the item. After the payments are over, you would do well to make use of the item until it falls apart. We tend to do this with our cars. We have gone many years with no car payments. Of course our 3 cars have a total of nearly 550,000 miles on them. At some point the maintenance on them will be more than a new car payment, and we will buy another car.

The Bornevan looking good after 15 years

Car leases are a trap set by car dealers to insure you never pay off a car and live without car payments. My recommendation is to buy a car and plan on driving it for 10 years.

Tithing, Or Some Semblance Thereof

Give money to your church. Work as hard as you can to give 10%, and do it before you buy a car or house, otherwise it will be impossible to do.

You Da' Man

You Time

Take care of yourself physically and spiritually. It becomes hard to care for yourself physically as the years roll by, but it will be a sign to your wife that you care enough about her to make sure you will be there for her later in life.

To take care of yourself physically, you will need to find a physical activity (other than sex) that you enjoy; otherwise you will not do it consistently. I have a hard time believing people actually enjoy jogging, so here are some other alternatives that I have tried that you may consider:

- Cycling
- Hiking or walking
- Racquetball
- Tennis
- Swimming (seasonal)
- Weight lifting (you will also need aerobic exercise to go with this).

It is as important to keep yourself fit spiritually, as it is physically. It has been important for me to keep my relationship with God intact. I do that by praying and reading. Praying is the way you talk to God. Pray every day. Pray even when you are too tired, and especially if you are too busy.

Reading is the way God talks to you. Listen when God talks to you as you read scripture. Read scripture or study theology every day. The more complicated the material the better. If you don't finish the day more confused than when you started, you didn't read hard enough material. You will need to build up to this; it is a growth opportunity.

Sneak Attack

Your kids are going to surprise you with questions about spirituality when you are least prepared for it, like when you are brushing your teeth or cooking dinner on the grill. I was once asked by one of my sons if he was "saved" while I had a mouth full of toothpaste. The only way to be ready for this is to have a firm grasp on your own spirituality, and always be ready to offer a defense of the faith.

Walk the Talk

Like it or not, you are going to define your kids' spirituality directly or indirectly. They should see you reading your Bible. It would be good if they could catch you praying. You must walk the talk; kids pick up pretty quickly on your hypocrisy.

Church is Good

Be involved in your church. You can teach Sunday school, sing in the choir, or serve on the missions committee. When the kids were young, we kept the nursery. It is good to have your kids in church. It is a safe place for them and they can develop lifelong friendships there. Be careful however not to let church take over your life to the exclusion of your family.

Framily

It is important to have friendships during your adulthood. We have been blessed to still have close friendships that originated in high school and college, which at this writing was 35 years ago. They are the 'Framily', our friends that are an extended part of our family, or as we like to say, the family we choose. It is an amazing gift to have a framily, and it does not happen without some effort. Fortunately the women of the framily make sure we all get together a couple of times a year.

In Conclusion

I was in college when I first met Mary Dell Sheppard, the woman who would someday be my wife. We were not in the same college, nor even in the same city. She was a friend of Vicky's who was the girlfriend of one of my best friends Gary. She was visiting Vicky one weekend at our college and we happened to meet. It seems improbable that we would even find each other, much less fall in love and get married. We had a two year, long distance relationship back before the days of email, cell phones and Facebook. We kept our relationship alive with phone calls and letter writing via the US Postal Service. I am convinced that it was God's plan that we end up together. As such, I take seriously the part of the wedding ceremony where the preacher says "What God has joined together, let no man separate." I don't want to be the one to cause us to separate.

When I first considered asking Mary Dell to marry me, I don't think I really understood the level of commitment I was about to make. All I knew was we could not stand to be separated from each other any longer and that we really wanted to be together. I asked her to marry me in the summer of 1979. Our parents were surprised, but supportive and offered dozens of reasons why we should wait to get married. None the less, love won out and we got married in the middle of my senior year in college on December 15, 1979.

When I said the words "I do" to Mary Dell during our wedding ceremony, I made many commitments to her. I committed to:

- Love her
- Protect her
- Provide for her

- Love our family
- Protect our family
- Provide for our family
- Be faithful to her

These commitments last until death separates us. Since Mary Dell agreed to "Love, honor and obey" me, I have a major responsibility to her to be worthy of her love and honor. We are still working on the obey part.

Being married is an awesome and overwhelming endeavor, but one full of joys. There have also been some less than joyful times along the way. Some of those less joyful times may have been averted had I been paying attention and acting like the husband I should have been. This book is a record of the mistakes I made and continue to make, and ways I have found to avoid them going forward. It is my hope that men who love their wife and family will find this book a useful tool to make their family life a happier one.

Glossary

Blissitudology

The study of domestic bliss-making is known as blissitudology. Bliss is achieved when you wife is happy.

Framily

The friends that are the family you choose comprise your framily. Many times your framily members are closer to you than your blood family members. Framily members are usually more fun as well.

Kids

The one(s) your wife talked you into fathering rather than having new houses and new cars (which you got later anyway). They are more expensive than Operation Desert Storm. If they still hug you when they are 12 years old, you will be the luckiest man alive.

Pets

The little animals running around your house are pets. They are differentiated from kids in that they are smarter and smell better. They are unable to hug, however.

Wife

The one who shares your life, who will be with you until death do you part.

About The Author

Bob Borneman resides in Cataula, Georgia with his wife of 32 years, Mary Dell, youngest son Walker, who is a senior at Harris County High School, and dogs Scarlett the attention-seeking Bassett Hound, and Millie the hyperactive three-legged mutt. Oldest son Adam is pastor of Second Presbyterian Church of Birmingham, Alabama. Daughter Koelling resides in Atlanta working in the public relations and media industry, as well as parenting foster dogs. Son Will continues as drummer with a new band and practices in his own home in Gainesville, Georgia. We are not sure if he continues to abide by the Silent Sunday rule, though we think probably not. Will is creating his own record label, and has his own recording studio.